ᴡ.

## Summary

Good-bye, rational culture! Let Guatemalan writer Alan Mills welcome you to the philosophy of tricksters. Follow him on a tour through indigenous mythology, classical education, and the literary canon, thoroughly mixed with hacking theory and with popular culture—from *Star Wars* and *Breaking Bad* to familiar figures like Bugs Bunny and El Zorro. Get to know Michael Jackson and David Bowie, Guy Fawkes and the *Popol Vuh*, the sacred book of the Maya-K'iche', through this fulminant essay on old and new strategies for resisting superpowers. If you don't yet know that the fox and the coyote can be read as symbols for destructive but simultaneously liberating deeds, if you haven't yet learned to see them as transcultural trickster-hipsters, reading this poetic, associative and witty panorama will open your eyes. Or, in the author's own words: "This open-source codex seeks to unite the contemporary traffickers of information with the smoke signals of their totemic animal." Mills currently lives in Berlin and Vienna.

Alan Mills

# **Hacking Coyote**
## Tricks for Digital Resistance

# Contents

## Quote

Wile E. [Coyote] is my *reality*.
Bugs Bunny is my *goal*.

**(Chuck Jones)**

# Coyote wanders through cyberspace

Liminal fox at Haus der Kulturen der Welt, Berlin Tiergarten.

We live in predatory times. We web users try to survive in the middle of a jungle, at times not so virtual, where hunters have intensified the stalking. Predators wearing the most varied cybernetic fur establish their monitoring circuits and extend their traps.

In both realms, the online world as well as in this outer space we call "reality", it seems that the hunting ground of the most powerful has widened to a frenetic rhythm, inversely proportional to the reduction of not a few of our prerogatives as citizens.

Hunting plus virtual stockbreeding: we are read, mapped, monitored, reviewed, controlled, programmed, directed like numbered cattle that will go to the slaughterhouse when the time comes; we are herded like electrical sheep unable to perceive the presence of danger.

We are jumping inside a mental barn. At times it seems that we wear an electronic tag that prevents us from moving without supervision or without allowing our creativity, our cyber navigations and our searches to be milked by hungry economic and political powers.

Our private data, our content on social media, our moribund ability to get free access to information, our clicks, our virtual identities and, ultimately, the different interconnected regions of our lives, have been in recent years under the siege of mercenaries acting with military efficiency. Oriented towards a portentous profitability in dollars or euros, their huge jaws swallow our freedoms and our rights as if they were just a bunch of emoticons or small Pokémon.

Anyone can see that we wander blindly while we pick the most poisonous flowers in the garden of calamities. We have become the stuffed turkey of a dinner to which they pretend to have invited us. We thank them because we are getting polished like a cannon ball meant for a weapon pointing against ourselves.

We feel like we are selling ourselves down the raging river that flows into La Chingada. But something inside us whispers that not everything is lost yet. It's getting down to the wire, folks, and yet we still have some small but vibrant hope, the cloud-figures in the sky indicate that a mischievous ancestral spirit wants to help us and hack the entangled network of this cyber war, the war for control of the Internet.

It's not a bird, it's not a plane, it's the spirit of Coyote!

The spectral beast has sunk its claws into the World Wide Web and has been digging a system of tunnels between the parallel dimensions of reality, virtuality, fiction and myth, in order to dismantle—and at the same time, celebrate—the farce of a Cyberspace that in its best days could have become truly democratic. In these fateful moments an old master of knowledge has reappeared among us: one that is part animal, part human, a little like a ghost and, equally, a code that enlightens us, inspires us, guides us and advises us during this debacle. This mutant messenger offers its knowledge to address the distorted virtual mirror of a terrible material catastrophe.

Coyote wanders decoding, taunting, challenging the sinister cyber totalitarianism of our time, while simultaneously blowing into our faces, shamelessly enough, a gentle caress of smoke from his fine Cuban cigar.

# OK, but who the f**k is Coyote?

Coyote is the master of chaos that makes his point by playing tricks, or through deception.

The teachings of this character are always as dubious as they are certain, as logical as illogical, as wise as ridiculous, as accurate as random. For some they come off as very clever, for others they seem very foolish. His speech is usually oriented towards paradox or looks toward disorder or entropy, since his purpose is to remind us that any situation can always be turned on its head, or that for every immanent system there exists a corresponding constant potential to be subverted.

This anti-hero bursts onto the scene when the Apollonian, rational, orderly, balanced and fair appearance of the world crumbles. He makes his bizarre triumphal entry precisely where the established order would have least expected him.

Some of his most powerful tricks are those that allow him to transform his identity, or to move fluidly between his equally animal, human, digital, spectral or holographic nature. Coyote has, for instance, the ability to snatch a hen from our coops before sliding out to make a cameo in the evening news. He can sneak just like a celebrity among the trending topics of social media, breaking with ease into the most commonly retold fairy tales, or shine in a television series with the highest rating of all time.

To confirm the latter we need only to recall—or to consult on YouTube, if we so desire—the episode of *The Simpsons* in which an incorrigible Homer Simpson is sent into a hallucinatory state after eating some red-hot Guatemalan Insanity Peppers in his chili.

The story goes that Homer has accepted the challenge of the Springfield's representative of order, Police Chief Wiggum, to eat a lot of Insanity Peppers brought from Quetzalacatenango. The result of this recklessness is a Homer Simpson with a burning mouth who enters a journey through other dimensions that will bring him out of reality, lead him to a psychedelic desert and position him temporarily on top of a pyramid of consciousness, a place where he will encounter a cosmic Coyote that speaks with the voice of Johnny Cash.

Coyote will tell Homer that his journey is a quest for knowledge, while at the same time motivating Homer to acquire a computer and find inner peace. Shortly after presenting him with a mysterious riddle, the fabulous little red animal simply disappears.

Coyote boldly moves between the dimensions of reality, fiction, dream, hallucination, and virtuality. He is one of the most popular sacred trickster transcultural avatars, analogous to characters in mythologies or various literatures known as Hermes, Legba, Pedro Urdemales, Inari or Puck.

He is the magician but also the clown of the party. He is a wicked alchemist. He is a playful elf. If he wishes, he can manifest as a poltergeist or as a smartphone that suddenly howls. When Siri makes a bad joke, take it easy—it may be that Coyote has taken possession of her voice.

This is the same little voice that advises the whistleblower that, on many occasions, the best way to survive is to play dumb.

He knows that the combination of being aware of one's own foolishness and playing the fool is a form of superior intelligence.

Coyote uses the same net(work) to fish for his food and to entangle his own legs. He mounts a Facebook profile to waste his invaluable time, but there it is, without even looking for it he finds the precious solution to a matter of life or death. Like the great Houdini, he prepares mortal traps for himself so that he can learn how to escape them alive.

We are facing the moralless moralist. The stories *Canis latrans* tells us may sound pompous or absurd until we begin to listen with ears free of any kind of prejudice or moralizing.

This same animal—often anthropomorphized, or wrapped in a jester's clothes—may appear as the protagonist or antagonist in the stories of the Navajo or the Sioux Indians: his role in these stories is always ambiguous as its fundamental mission is to communicate, for those who are reading or listening, certain vital pieces of knowledge not transmittable in any other way.

The coyote is a trafficker of ancient secrets or very important conundrums.

His species is an Olympic medalist in the sport of survival. Coyote's fearsome ferocity allows him to hunt alone or in groups and he never shies away from fighting other vermin, including those who pose great danger. Yet he understands very well when to retreat.

Some even say that some coyotes know how to play dead by copying the classic trick of the opossum, and some say that he knows how to hack the operating system of the enemy, to encrypt his data, to use a false identity, to maintain anonymity, to downsize, or to cross-dress in accordance with the conditions of a system, or according to the needs of the historical moment.

This restless canid represents the genius of trans-formations.

As already mentioned, Coyote embodies one hy-postasis of the trickster archetype, the divine trickster, the transhistoric rogue. It is one of the many faces of the global shape shifter, the same being who assumes various identities, various bodies or inter-faces, particular characteristics and different names according to each tradition where it is taken into ac-count, becoming Loki, Leprechaun, Reynard the Fox, or San Simon.

This transcultural little avatar does not care to be considered hero or villain, saint or devil.

It is said that although he likes luxury, he often sympathizes with the needy.

It is also known that the energy of Coyote can sometimes manifest as Donnie Darko's grisly rabbit Frank, or the Joker, or the fiery hero Gokú throwing dragon spheres.

Open secret: Gokú is a pop upgrade from Monkey King, the ancient Chinese trickster reloaded for the masses.

Our dear shape shifter can equally take the form of a fox turning up its nose at the bait in some Chinese forest, or the disturbing raven that whispers *Nevermore* at the window of the romantic poet, or the fake fox—for actually is a red panda—of Mozilla Firefox's logo. Gossips say Coyote can even take, even if for short dreamlike moments, the form of the artist formerly known as Prince or the face of some iconic founder of Tor.

It is not to say that all these characters are one and the same, but rather that they all act or behave in similar ways within the most diverse range of cultural frameworks. You could say that each character develops more strongly one or more of the many defining aspects of the ancestral operator of the tricks, the cherished archetypical trickster.

One of his most persistent features, for example, is his voracious sexual appetite, a very intense drive this bold desperado must learn to master. Another of his constant features is his crooked sense of humor. Reading the contemporary Bible on the subject: *Trickster Makes This World: Mischief, Myth and Art*, by the author Lewys Hyde, is the best way to deepen your understanding of the characterology and the many manifestations of the trickster.

Within the cyber realm, the coyote-esque energy usually manifests in a computer pirate who sometimes descends to the deep web and right there sells some weird products to spectral consumers, takes the more or less fat profits in bitcoins, makes a suspect barter here and there, keeps browsing aimlessly and, one way or another, manages to overcome all persecutions, whether real or imaginary, until the police are finally left empty-handed.

Coyote is both the animal incarnation of the creative powers of the earth and the living deployment of the necessary amount of cunning that will save us from the most overwhelming telluric forces. Through avatar after avatar left behind and electronic trap after electronic trap dismantled, the trickster teaches us that, forced to choose, it is preferable to be considered a chicken than to be forced to endure a virtual cavity search by, let's say, the NSA.

In his role of techno-shaman he likes to combine the wisdom of indigenous elders with the zany knowledge of the cybernetics pundits, since he understands that technology and psychedelia can go hand in hand when it comes to hacking into the deepest secrets of the psyche. Under this same techno-shamanic identity he suggests the possibility of circumventing joyfully any tribulations we may find along our journey through the realm of shadows. Laughingly he predicts that one day the enlightenment finally will come to us, and only then will we accept that the healthiest strategy for navigating successfully between the grey jungle of the panoptic Web and the colorful and bloody desert of the hyperreal will be to acquire some coyote-esque powers right away.

Coyotes are recognized to be the most effective at slipping past any surveillance device, bypassing any border checkpoint and sneaking past gatekeepers of all sorts.

Coyote's fascination with crossroads is legendary. Coyote is the wild hacker that goes in and out of the lettered city. Coyote scent-marks the Smart Cities Dystopia. He traffics news of varying size in various directions. It is not by chance that an author, Gabriella Coleman, has built the most interesting semiotic bridge between tricksters and the hacktivist group 'Anonymous', or between the trolls of mythology and the unbearable Internet trolls.

Coyote knows how to troll the beautiful people, the powerful ones. She is also an escapist drag queen. He is a cryptographer clown. She is a punk shaman. He's an elf playing cards.

Our antihero loves gambling. He wants the world to be dynamic, mobile, collapsible, just as much as he loathes the rigid environments, the enclosed spaces or the stone structures. She's a tunnel excavator. He opens exchange pathways.

Our animal spirit is always looking for ways to allow the flow of information to move between the most diverse actors in the social game, and also promotes a kind of carnivalesque distribution of goods; he pushes forward a constant (if not necessarily fair) distribution of stuff, which is often the result of error, fluke, accident, or failure. He dislikes the great hoarders of information and knowledge working only for the sake of the private profit, those greedy holders of the creative wealth of the world, whether analog or online, mainly because these people make the game more boring.

For make no mistake: the coyote may be playing but he is known to be severe. Compassion is not his cup of tea and he does not pay any attention to moral behavior, as we may already have come to realize or intuited. His mission is both to keep alive the Promethean fire of wit and imagination, and to cause the blackout that will allow us to tear down those walls that prevent the cheerful and chaotic flow of knowledge, ideas, creations, people, goods and images.

The teachings of this ancient spirit roam equally the dusty roads in North, Central and South America, or the invisible electronic highways penetrating the five continents as plasma. His mercurial fluidity allows him to include his message in any oral story among the nomads of the sub-Saharan steppes under the figure of the fox or of any other animal messenger, or to fluctuate over the most unexpected searches undergone by some Ugandan user of the Mercury browser, or to cross-dress as the arsonist masked villain of some British comic.

*fluidity*

When circumstances are favorable Coyote can even infiltrate international Internet and New Media conferences in Berlin—let's say some multimedia sessions in the popular, crowded and trendy re:publica and Transmediale—with the aim of questioning inequality in information, the digital divide between the First World countries and the Global South.

Coyote's rambunctious and irreverent nature, coupled with his innate taste for or interest in renewing the distribution of the goods of the world, can transform him into a staunch critic of digital colonialism.

# Hacking the Empire: digital colonialism vs. enlightened coyote-ism

Guy Fawkes mask and Heisenberg figurine.

In the parallel reality of a certain series of Hollywood science fiction movies, the insurgent forces are *Star Wars* preparing a rebellion against the evil Empire from bases that turn out to be, in reality, the temples of the Mayan city of Tikal.

The "star-wars" of the ancient Maya—as the huge conflicts between their city-states were called—have been redefined by the mass culture of the late twentieth century as a brand new *Star Wars*, in which, by the way, the Maya themselves are conspicuous in their absence.

There is a relationship perhaps not entirely coincidental or unrelated between the fictional clash of powers in the film *Star Wars IV: A New Hope* and the social forces that face each other in the real world. It is as if a series of fractal paradoxes are bound and put in the different dimensions captured by our minds: the ruins of an ancient fallen empire serve as a backdrop against which the Empire of today opens up an imagined space to certain subversive impulses rather undesirable if it materializes, let's say, among exactly those indigenous peoples subjected to quasi-colonial economic relations today.

In a similar way, material colonialism is reflected or expressed in the asymmetries of the contemporary digital world: on the ruins of an original Web that promised universal access to knowledge, a block of computer consortia has been mounted that, while they can simulate a true alternative candor, as in the specific case of the Silicon Valley companies in the United States, at the same time make it quite clear that their post-industrial motors revolve around alienation and dispossession of Internet users worldwide, all this at the same pace with which they are systematizing, classifying, manipulating and making profitable our data, interests and ideas, limiting utopian open access to information, making the web a less neutral space every day.

The negative impact of this neo-colonial structure of cyber power is even greater, of course, for the citizens of the countries that are weakest in the production and consumption of technology, who at the end of the day barely benefit from the virtues of this Internet now virtually kidnapped by the transnationals.

## Colonialism and ancestral digital resistance

But if one can talk about how material colonialism is reproduced in the virtual space, it is also possible to speak of a political resistance to digital oppression.

Resistance in the digital world: Let's use the Mayan culture as an example. Let's take a look at its transhistorical resistance to a particular way of colonization.

As we all know, the European invasion of the "Abya Yala" territories (North America, Central America and South America) began a few centuries ago: the Caribbean, Guarani, Mayan, Mapuche, Inca, Aymara, Taino, Aztec people, etc.—though all were very different, both culturally and in their levels of technical development—were all subjected to the European Imperialist powers. A long and painful process of colonization began, and is still being resisted today.

What is rarely taken into account, however, is that the colonizer settlement involved the collision of two or more writing systems. And one also rarely thinks about the clash of the two calculation systems involved in the colonization process: while the digital culture of the colonial West is based on the number 10, the digital culture of the Maya has always been based on the twenty digits comprising the fingers and toes. It's clear, then, that the colonization of some American peoples included the clash between the vigesimal and the decimal system: a digital clash in the making.

In the end, or rather at the end of many long and bloody battles, the decimal system was imposed as a hegemonic throughout the "new world". However, it is crucial to note that calculation is not a form of knowledge that came to Abya Yala thanks to Europeans, and neither is, in an absolute sense at least, the *techne* of writing, because although it is true that among the Mayans—from the ancients to those who met the conquistadores—hieroglyphic and logo-syllabic writing were restricted to the ruling and priestly caste, such epistemic technology had full existence in their collective imagination, as shown in books painted on amate bark and other artifacts.

Let's pause here to open a brief parenthesis: we must not look at this elitism of the Mesoamerican as such a surprising phenomenon, especially when it's taken into consideration that programming (just by way of example), is a defining characteristic of the present time, in spite of the fact that only a very small percentage of people across the globe are capable of writing code.

Closing this parenthesis and moving forward, it can be said that colonial domination imposed a new temporal regime (calendar) over the conquered territories, as well as a regime of knowledge production (alphabetic writing, then also the press), and a restrictive system of control and access to information (inquisition, etc.).

The conflict was not only between the Western literate culture and the oral culture prevalent among Amerindians, which is the common simplification; techniques of native writing were gradually cornered, too, or became obsolete due to violence, or the brutal work regime. The native people remain alienated from their own formal systems of ideological production, their aboriginal knowledge has been obliterated, their "painted books" were confiscated, their codes or codex were largely destroyed. Their transmedia textualities—in textiles, sculptural, performative, musical, or in human supports—and their calendars often had to go into hiding and receive the protection of resistance movements.

## Maya-hackers & Anonymous

Faced with the prospect of the imminent destruction of Aboriginal knowledge, the first Maya-hackers emerged.

In order to protect their ancestral knowledge, the clandestine figure of Diego Reynoso appeared. Both native and nobleman (or apparently so), he learns the code of the oppressor and transcribes to the Latin alphabet the sacred book of the Maya-K'iche', a compilation of knowledge that is vital to the community.

Diego Reynoso has been identified as the first transcriber of an unknown hieroglyphic manuscript of the sacred book of the Maya- K'iche', and this is to be noted even though his name remains obscured by a rather fuzzy, hazy, barely distinguishable quality, because there is very little documentation to show that he even existed at all. His identity is indeed so problematic that some people speculate "Diego Reynoso" could have been the "codename" used by one or more hidden transcribers.

This idea of a phantom transcriber is as interesting to consider as the issue of the authorship of the sacred book itself: yes, Diego Reynoso is the elusive transcriber of the *Popol Vuh*, but the author of the sacred text of the Maya- K'iche' remains anonymous.

That's it, the author of the *Popol Vuh* is Anonymous.

- 25 -

It can be inferred, of course, that such anonymity would protect the author or authors from a potential persecution while simultaneously maintain the necessary quota of secrecy and mystery, aspects that will eventually increase the symbolic power of the text.

According to the Guatemalan poet Luis Cardoza y Aragón, the author of the *Popol Vuh* would have been "a magic elder, just like the heroes of its stories." And to the previous argument we could also add the idea that such an ineffable author may have been as much a god as a human being, particularly when taken into consideration that he accomplished the divine trick of keeping his identity a complete enigma.

Authorship is sacred, that is, is protected, because it is an action of all and none. The author or authors of the *Popol Vuh*, i.e., the book of the community, the Pop Book, operated within an anonymity that works as a cultural form of resistance put up against the progress of the taxonomic and predatory colonial civilizing power.

Similarly to what happens with the contemporary hacktivist collective hidden under the mask of Guy Fawkes, the authorial stamp 'Anonymous' will become a stratagem that protects the true identity and location—or to put it in modern terms, the privacy—of the mystical primary drafters of the Mayan-K'iche' sacred text.

It remains clear that this old trick of anonymity, which on the one hand acts as protection from inquisitorial persecution and on the other side mystifies the writing, is not a trick known only by the Mayan priests but rather a common heritage from the most diverse authors of sacred texts, mystical documents or heretical books that spread from time immemorial all over the world.

We are talking about an old trick that the old Hermes and the old Coyote have in common. We are speaking of a kind of textual masking which could be seen today as a precedent for the ethics governing Anonymous—those collectives of hackers and pranksters who are today a thorn in the heart of power—or as a transtemporal challenge to the modern notion, still so restrictive, of private property and intellectual property.

## Coyote strikes back

As suggested earlier in this book, the contemporary figure of the hacker may be related to the ancestral figure of the trickster or the Coyote from original peoples, of which multiple variations appear in mythical tales from around the world. It remains especially powerful among North American and Latin American indigenous peoples, from the Eskimos in the north to the Mapuches in the south.

Coyote—sometimes depicted as rabbit, opossum, crow, or fox—is a teacher who shuttles knowledge between different worlds or different realities. He uses guile or mischief as a tactic; he is a little devil seeking flaws in the systemic network. He is an amoral being that puts the institutional normalcy on hold: it is not by chance that the people who transport-traffic individuals between borders in Latin America are called "coyotes".

He appears, as the musical genius Robert Johnson attested in his day, at the crossroads, in the crosswalk, or at the most delicate junctures—just at that point where it becomes necessary to choose a route or overcome a limitation. It is no wonder that this book equates hackers, tricksters and Coyote.

Such categories describe liminal beings who survive thanks to their constant mobility, and thanks to a perpetual state of "dynamic ambiguity," as the American novelist Thomas Pynchon called it: a state that, according to the enigmatic novelist, remembers or metaphorizes the Heisenberg uncertainty principle.

*Maya shape-shifting trixter example*

In the case of the Maya, one of the most remarkable trickster shape-shifter archetype configurations appears in the form of the twin heroes of the sacred book of the K'iche'. The protagonists of the *Popol Vuh* are twin siblings—or two aspects of a single being, according to some—called Hunahpú and Ixbalanqué that embody the trickster-hacker figure of Coyote in the book. Or to put it more accurately, they are the ones who become Coyote (Hunahpú Utiú) and Opossum or Tacuacín (Hunahpú Uuch), while at the same time disguising themselves as homeless people or street magicians. Such are the trickster-hackers of the Maya-K'iche'.

Throughout the holy book they avoid a number of trials until they triumph in the oppressor's own territory: Xibalba, a dark place reigned by the dead, the petrified, the rigid, a place where mobility is punished.

Hunahpú and Ixbalanqué delve into the Xibalba cyberspace to defeat the lords of shadow who have challenged them to play. These dark lords prevent access to the light—a metaphor for knowledge or consciousness—and thus block the brotherhood and friendship between the different beings who live in the community. This is why the community creates or imagines the god-heroes able to overcome the lords of Xibalba.

The twins achieve their final victory through the use of disguises, tricks, small enchantments, metamorphoses, jokes and deception. These actions allow them to decipher the language of Xibalba, i.e., the language of fear, and so they are, through their playful wandering, gaining a language with which they get to communicate with the forces of nature and survive thanks to its help.

Coyote heroes advance fearless in their journey through the abyss, accepting challenges like children who modify their leaping to fit a game of hopscotch, or like the reckless smugglers Han Solo and his animal companion Chewbacca—notorious and, therefore, not entirely reliable shape shifters—who are able to face the evil Empire without major drama. The twins take up the challenge of the dark side as foxes innocently accept the game of survival in the forest, with the result that our heroes are allowed to absorb defeats—as a matter of fact, the twins are defeated in their first foray into Xibalba—as a unique way to hone their tricks, strategies, and tactics, paving the way for arrival at a supreme victory that they pursue with determination but without obstinacy; their mood is, rather, a cheerful or burlesque one, and at times gives off the impression that they are jumping into battle without really knowing why.

According to the mythical story, when Hunahpú and Ixbalanqué finally and happily triumph over the evil empire, they rise into the sky and are transformed into the moon and the sun: the reading eyes the community uses to decipher the sacred text of life, two eyes that contemplate the mutable beauty of hope, the ripe fruit matured in the process of their own resistance to oppression.

## Lighting a candle for hackers

All this is obviously important to understanding that having access to an open, unbiased Internet is an inalienable right that is worth fighting for. If you have an Internet connection right now, try searching "Popol Vuh". In any browser on any computer anywhere in the world, you have the ability to draw on the wisdom of the Maya-K'iche' in the most varied formats, whether these be writings, audio, video, or multimedia.

Due to the archaic "cultural hacking" operation developed by a certain Diego Reynoso, we now have easy access to the sacred book of the Maya-K'iche': an anonymously authored compilation, sacred, collective, an extraordinary story that presents a series of survival strategies that everyone may take advantage of. Because the *Popol Vuh* is by now translated into many languages, native young people, mestizos, individuals from western cultures, alien beings from distant galaxies, indeed everyone can recreate it, reinterpret it, and get fluently in touch with this knowledge in different variations and languages.

The culture of hacking and/or decoding closed knowledge is an ancient practice that ensures the survival of human communities like the Maya, but the values of Hunahpú and Ixbalanqué still prevail in modern times. Hacking the oppressor's code guarantees the longevity of knowledge of the oppressed by providing them with the ability to keep the record of their struggles, traditions, and stories. The main goal of hacking is survival: in order not to remain alienated from the world trade, you enter the key code for other versions of the world, so the key code is modified to include marginalized codex.

Thus cultural hacking shows its relevance, its timeliness. Maintaining open access to all sources of cultural information makes possible the creation of richer societies, full of greater choice. A global society such as ours, wrapped in such a tremendous financial and social crisis, needs to circulate critical values that allow for its transformation, change, and renewal—this is why it is necessary to struggle in favor of allowing these acts of rebellion to keep circulating or to circulate more. It is imperative for our global community to incorporate the values of the twin heroes in order to overcome the lords of shadow that block free access to the light of knowledge.

Hack, hack and hack some more. Do not forget that it is a transtemporal set of artisanal and modern hacking operations that has allowed Hunahpú and Ixbalanqué values to survive in the contemporary world. And I am not speaking here only of hacking the alphabetical code that made the transcription of the sacred book of the Maya possible, but also of the ritual syncretism, the indigenous hacking of the Catholic Church performative code—one of the highest ideological instances in the world dominated by the West—which has led to the baroque mixture of beliefs between the conquerors and the conquered, between the oppressors and the oppressed in Latin America. Syncretism has been a model used by the subordinate peoples to re-shape the ideology itself that has shaped the colonial process, creating the living theater of a new belief.

For example, in many countries, both indigenous and mestizo Latin American peoples pay homage to figures such as folk saints that embody these ambiguous, androgynous, transitive and transformational values: the trickster or Coyote values. The values of the Hero Twins of the *Popol Vuh*. This usually takes the form of people or sanctified characters of the community whose existence may not have been verified. In Central America, to focus on just one case, several communities worship Maximón (also called San Simon), a mystical embodiment of some of the archetypical trickster or shape-shifter values. Like the North American Coyote, Maximón likes to smoke and drink, he plays pranks, he is a saint who is also a devil, a deity who embodies the chaotic duality of nature.

Maximón

Mask portraying the poet Maximón.

Maximón is a Mayan spirit just like the twins Hunahpú and Ixbalanqué but he also possesses the fierce-
ness of the Spanish conquistador who knows how to
succeed. He is a shrewd rebel but also a severe lord of
the underworld, or a ruthless agent of the dark side
of the Force: do not forget that, in the end, the heroes
Luke and Leia Skywalker are the children of the vil-
lainous Darth Vader and Hunahpú and Ixbalanqué are
the children of Ixkik, a native of Xibalba.

   Maximón/San Simon is indigenous but also European and he is also mestizo. He is more Spanish than
the Spanish and is more indigenous than the indigenous because he integrates all the elements in an
even more imaginative way. Maximón/San Simon
owes to his sort of open-source rite the possibility of
mixing Catholic with native beliefs, also adding some
popular culture elements, even integrating contemporary references to American mass culture, i.e. the
transnational and neo-colonial culture of capitalism.
San Simon/Maximón officiates as an unofficial saint
who articulates the different worldviews of a social
space that has inevitably become mixed. He does it

through a patchwork, ever-changing, very dynamic ritual, open to everything, that enables him to keep his transitive, negotiator, weaver values in action.

We see, then, a coyote-hacker sacralization that helps to keep the outsider success stories alive and the rogue rebel values circulating. The logic of the impoverished Central American communities is that if structures of power prevent their access to proper education, free and uncensored Internet, and so on, then their heroic bandits, those who have always managed to hack into the centers of power and get away with it, will survive through the ritual.

The folk saints' ritual allows their legendary stories and unprecedented miracles to guide the path of their devotees, often outsiders themselves. And while it is true that such miraculous stories cannot be proven, at least from a rational point of view, they are vital for those who believe in them, because these miracles are living stories that provide inspiration to individuals and communities who resist the pressures and oppressions, both material and virtual, of old and new colonialism.

# Why should we listen to Coyote?

It is not the intention of this book to alarm anyone—
or perhaps it is—but some scholars at some presti-
gious universities have announced that the world has
entered a new phase of mass extinction. The most recent of these events happened 65 million years ago,
remember?, it was that bright moment when a super
Poké Ball broke the Earth's atmosphere and roasted
the dinosaurs over the coals. Well, the point is that
according to the oracles of the rationalists, now it is
our turn, we super-evolved primates, we cyber-pri-
mates, to become the unfortunate main dish of the
cosmic barbecue.

Man, it's not so hard to imagine that our flesh
could surpass the lizard's in terms of taste, which,
like frog legs, in the best case scenario tastes like
chicken—though perhaps it should be taken into account that some Amazonian gourmet once said that
humans are pork flavored. You can keep saying that
God does not play dice, if you like, or whatever you
want, as long as you don't try to deny that, over the
years, that divine bastard Hannibal Lecter has been
refining his palate.

The most fucked up thing is that now we can't
even blame the cosmic vagaries—as the dinosaur's
spokespeople have done—because everything rather
indicates that the burning meteorite that will put
everything to an end is just ourselves. You don't even
need to have a Hubble telescope, you can observe the
signals that precede the aforementioned mass extinction with your naked eye: we have deteriorated the
environment so much that both 40% of amphibious

species and 20% of mammalian species have been swept off the face of the earth during the last 100 years; we have devastated countless kilometers of forest; hunger is plaguing at least 800 million humans as a result of an unsustainable economic system where 1% of the human population accounts for 90% of the wealth and where transnationalism operates as a new empire that rules with an iron cyber fist.

We don't even need zodiac signs to announce it, scientists themselves are saying that the solar orbit has brought the sun to the exact point (the "interstellar danger zone") in which it was during that remote time when terrible lizards ran this cheerful dump. Maybe the tone's already getting too Aquarian, or new age-y, but I can't help it, there is no other way to say it: the earth needs to tell us something and it seems more than just a hunch that she's chosen the coyote as her messenger.

As we all know, Coyote is a bandit, he does nothing for the sake of appearances—we are one of his predators, don't forget—and never helps others for free. That is to say that Coyote is not providing this service out of good will, that's sure. What will happen is that if things continue as they are, most likely his species, too, will be included inside of this new special mass extinction package.

*amoral*

The golden beast wants to save his own skin, that is why he's manifesting himself in dreams, that is why he seeps into pop songs, or into postmodern essays, or into Catholic rituals, or into a television series, or into our sacrosanct social media, or into cartoons, it's why we find Coyote all over Cyberspace: a couple of clicks here and there and we will see him jump to life again before our eyes. And then one day you go to bed and dream that you are the German artist Joseph Beuys. You recognize this new identity because you are tucked into the room with a coyote. The animal looks you in the eye, explores your performance. Gradually comes into your mind. Then he exits your head again but he keeps looking, telling you something you do not know yet how to decipher.

Trickster/rabbit graffiti in Hufelandstrasse, Berlin Prenzlauer Berg.

Only Coyote knows us better than the Google algorithm. We understand, he is well aware that, like him, what we want most is to survive, by all means, he knows that deep down what moves us forward is the idea of perpetuating our genetic code, yes, a dark desire if not properly taken and expanded into the collective code.

We are now facing the challenge of becoming one with Coyote, as the mythical Don Juan suggested to Carlos Castaneda as a way of getting a coherent perspective on earth messages, nature messages, nagual messages.

And perhaps the global multiplication of Coyote signals is a response to this need for integration.

In his various guises, the beast bubbles up everywhere. Just as tricksters usually appear in literary stories to motivate a transformation in the protagonist, or to bring about a change of narrative direction, the collective encounter with the symbolic Coyote perhaps suggests that it is necessary to recognize the present darkness and to start up an intense process of economic, social, digital and therefore political conversion that will lead to an immediate restoration and reinvention of natural, human and virtual ecosystems.

If we are bold enough we might even come to the same conclusion that Coyote communicated to Joseph Beuys: one must hack one's own consciousness in order to break the barriers that prevent reprogramming the algorithm of our vital story itself, or (which is the same) altering the narrative of one's own fiction, and this may not be only an individual action. It may even mean acting as small representative fractals for the whole species.

# San Coyote: drug dealer and spiritual hacker

## Breaking Coyote

Now we will try to conduct a panoramic flight over the phenomenon of Coyote's sacralization, by way of a creative or experimental hypothesis: let's imagine the lead character of the popular television series *Breaking Bad*, the equally popular Heisenberg or Walter White, as a "coyote-esque" figure that incorporates some features of coyotes themselves as well as other typical traces of the so-called "folk saints".

The idea is to continue scanning for Coyote's presence winding and wandering through the multiple layers of the contemporary transmedial experience, this time through the analysis of certain aspects perhaps unnoticed in one of the most award-winning American series of recent times, *Breaking Bad*, a series that tells the story of a "nobody" who becomes one of the top American drug dealers and an evil genius. And all this happens thanks to being confronted with imminent death, following the announcement of terminal cancer.

## Coyote inside Walter White

*Breaking Bad*, at times, wants to integrate into the world of television some of Coyote's afterworlds. The presence of indigenous or pre-Hispanic motifs, for example, covers the series from start to finish as a smoke shadow: Smoking Indian decorations in the courtyard of Walter White's family residence; the Pontiac Aztek the protagonist will drive for most of the series; that service station called "Big Chief" where—during Season 3—Walter's partner, his fellow trickster Jesse Pinkman, will lead a naive and stocky dependent down the garden path; they all are small nods to or traces of such a presence.

Behind the world we see there is another nearly invisible world, the world of Coyote, the same world the urban middle class, the class that feels as if it is the depository for the process of modernization, chooses to ignore. What is essential is invisible to the eyes: perhaps this is what the perpetual desert paintings that appear in various living rooms scattered throughout the whole geography of the series are intended to make us remember. If you take a slow look at these pictures, they will bring to mind the dusty horizons of Wile E. Coyote.

Coyote inhabits the borders of our bourgeois lifestyle: besieges the city just from that secluded place, lost in desert hills, where the drug is cooked at the beginning of the story, the same space where much later, at the end of the series, a circle will be drawn closed with the burial of all the money accumulated by Heisenberg/Walter White throughout his rather short career as a drug dealer.

But Coyote was always there. Recall that Walter White began his "spiritual awakening" as a criminal when he lied about his first weekend cooking crystal meth in industrial quantities: in Episode 7, Season 1, he tells Skyler, his wife, he has gone to a "healing ceremony" in a Navajo sweat lodge. And later he will tell Skyler that the smell of cooked methamphetamine he could not remove from his clothing is just the aroma of the "sacred Navajo herbs".

A believer in the indigenous people's spirituality might say that if the healing ceremony had actually been practiced, the soul of Walter White would not have moved to the dark side, that is, Walter would not have become the criminal Heisenberg.

This is nothing more than a guess, of course, but comparable to the argument of believers in the welfare state who say that this pusillanimous chemistry professor would never have become a feared criminal if the government had paid his medical expenses when he was diagnosed with lung cancer.

### San Walter White

In October 2013, the royal burial of a fictional character was held in Albuquerque, New Mexico.

Walter White's funeral—organized shortly after his death during the final episode of *Breaking Bad*—gathered more than two hundred people and raised about $17,000 that was delivered, as a kind of postmodern offering, to a homeless support organization.

This unique event was devised by a man named Michael Baird, who claimed, at the same time the fake funeral was held, never to have seen a single chapter of the popular AMC series.

Michael Baird would make the decision to hold the funeral after being moved by an account of *Breaking Bad* from the janitor of his own restaurant, Vernom's Steakhouse. It is not entirely clear, however, if he was touched by hearing the tragedy of a fictional character recounted as if it were a real person, or if his business sense told him he could capitalize on the media phenomenon. Chances are that there was a bit of both.

However, beyond the obvious intention of promoting his restaurant as a tourist destination in the state of New Mexico, under the auspices of the world-famous series and its characters, it's noteworthy that Michael Baird reacted to an oral narrative: the story told to him by his employee, combined (according to own Baird's statements to the press) with the remarkable effect that the TV series had on the people around him, were sufficient for him to believe in the importance of the "life and miracles" of a rather modest chemistry professor turned drug dealer and, ultimately, also held up as a martyr or cultural hero.

It's even arguable that the owner of Vernom's Steakhouse organized the burial as an act of faith, because he believed in something without having to see it for himself on the screen.

The end of this intrusion of television fiction in the real world would be marked by the appearance of a note of prayer for the eternal repose of Walter White's soul, published in the *Albuquerque Journal*, coupled with the sudden pilgrimage of hundreds of fans from the most diverse places, who visited the grave installed temporarily in the city cemetery as if they were devotees coming to honor the life of a saint.

### Serial saints

Folk saints are those "miraculous souls" not recognized by the Catholic Church. Interestingly, many folk saint stories had similar beginnings to the (potential) Walter White folk cult in Albuquerque. The story of the origins of a popular saint usually has a nebulous aura, because the central figure's documented life and information contributed by the testimonies of the locals are confused. The place where the saint has begun to manifest becomes sacred, that is, starts to generate reports of miracles.

But this happened outside of *Breaking Bad*'s space, in the real world. Inside the series, however, the only time Walter White is called "a saint" is when the corrupt lawyer Saul Goodman appoints him ironically as "the saint of cancer" because they associate to launder money, using as their front the web page that Walter's son has set up in his honor in order to raise money for his costly treatment. Walter White, the false saint of cancer, performs here a classic trickster trick, advised by a professional trickster: Saul Goodman.

Fake saints or real devils, everything depends on the point of view of the observer.

At another point in the series, an enigmatic image appears: Jesus Malverde, the folk saint of northern Mexico, who is said to protect drug traffickers, coyotes (or migrant smugglers), prostitutes and criminals in exchange for their veneration.

The statuettes of Jesus Malverde burst in Episode 7 of the second season, accompanied by a video of the narcocorrido band Los Cuates de Sinaloa (in English: Sinaloa Twins) performing "Negro y Azul," in which the most representative and eloquent line goes, "That homie's [Heisenberg, it is clear] already dead, he just doesn't know it yet."

That is, the oral telling—essential in bringing folk saints to life—here has taken the form of an audiovisual narcocorrido that reveals a transposition, almost a mirror, between Jesus Malverde and Walter White images, leaving the impression that both characters—despite being antagonistic inside the corrido—would be more closely related than you might think at first glance: both have dark mustaches, both are brave and cunning, both have rebelled against the established order and legality, and both are popular among the marginalized: Malverde among the poor in Mexico and Heisenberg among Americans addicted to crystal meth (and as we have seen, even among citizens addicted to the television series).

Critics of the folk saints often point to the inability to document their existence historically, and accuse them of being part of a mythological collective illusion that just leads to superstitions. Such accusations, however, do not seem to worry the devotees who continue to make offerings and give testimony of the miracles, so that one could infer that they care more about the allegorical quality of their narrative construction than its factuality or validity. The story of the miracle gives meaning to the very existence of the devotees, and in this way they find a new narrative coherence for their own life. And this new coherence, I would daresay, is their faith's cornerstone.

This phenomenon of popular devotion, if viewed carefully, is quite similar to the one showed by the *Breaking Bad* fans who came to lay flowers at the real grave of a character whose existence was avowedly fictional.

As already mentioned, the folk cults thrive on mystery stories where the real and the fictional are mixed, in the same way that Heisenberg shapes his reputation as high-flying outlaw throughout the various seasons of the series, walking a line between urban legends and the imprint of his real actions on the fictional city.

All this makes Walter White/Heisenberg not only to look a bit like the Mexican Malverde but also like several Latin American folk saints such as the Guatemalan San Simon—also called "Maximón" by the indigenous—and the Argentinian Gauchito Gil, all of them also identified as miraculous souls that accompany the fate of the marginalized and persecuted.

It could be argued that all these saints are merely the various transfigurations of the same entity—a Hermes derived from the Greek and/or the Egyptian alchemist Hermes Trismegistus, mixed with their indigenous counterparts, most probably; it is not by chance that philosopher Michel Serres has established Hermes and Harlequin as melting pot and cultural mixing symbols—the same spirit that acquires different cultural characteristics in different regions where their religion is based. And such a condition, of course, would link these saints with our beloved Coyote.

As if that were not enough, the fact that the money raised by Walter White's funeral has been offered up to those in need constitutes another resonance between the television character and the dynamics of syncretic folk rites, since these alternative spiritualities, quite rooted in Latin America, moreover, often serve as negotiators and redistributive expressions that create carnivalesque spaces of exchange, often as community compensators to their abandonment by the state.

Cults like that of Jesus Malverde, accused of being the saint of drug dealers, move in the coordinate of the challenge to a law that lacks social legitimacy.

The popular spirituality moves in the orbit of the "baroque's second law" spoken by Ecuadorian philosopher Bolívar Echeverría: a kind of a dramatization of reality that redefines and supersedes reality, an imaginative response of the working classes to the rigid order of a modernization process that has not always considered them.

The cult of the outlaw, or of those who are positioned in an intermezzo between the legal and the illegal, acts as a performative questioning of the existing law as fixed or static. The popular consecration of the bandits seeks to make the provision of penalties for members of the subaltern communities more flexible, and denote the intrinsically unjust hierarchy of power, or the moral imprecision in the source of all wealth. It is a balancing act for the plebeian criminals to acquire the same status as the elite criminals.

During times of economic and political crisis the idolatry and sanctification of bandits is something usual. And this is not a trait reserved for Latin America; in fact it is easy to recall, just by way of example, the rise of figures like the undaunted Americans Bonnie and Clyde during the Great Depression of the world economy in the 1930s.

As the great Eric Hobsbawm develops in his book *Bandits*: in front of an unjust law, or before an anachronistic norm, or faced to a despotic authority, or simply faced with a social situation in which the State fails to fulfill its standard functions, social bandits become popular heroes, and the greater their transgression the stronger and more loved they always will be.

The appearance of Malverde in *Breaking Bad* fits this Hobsbawmian dictum. His explosive entrance is a response to a hunt for Mexican drug-dealers organized by a police establishment that boasts of its somewhat corrupt or, at least, unorthodox procedures.

At first glance—assuming that the logic of folk rituals runs through the series' own narrative mechanisms—one could also assume that the disrespectful or mocking invocation of Malverde made by the policemen under the slogan of "know your enemy" causes the bloody death of these same boastful DEA agents and also causes serious injuries to Hank Schroeder, one of Walter White's main antagonists.

Despite the latter, the veneration of an enemy is a ritual practice that can be effective in accordance with the logic of folk saints: in Guatemala, for instance, some say that the indigenous who dressed Maximón/San Simon in the clothes of the military managed to expel the army of their communities during the worst years of the armed conflict in the early eighties, besides the fact of San Simon himself being usually associated with the cruel conquistador Pedro de Alvarado.

This phenomenon, the ritual integration of an enemy, is probably related to what Jungians call the "confrontation with the shadow" (and its subsequent integration), an essential step to achieve so-called "individuation" or what could also be called: awareness, consciousness.

But if we return to the series, we will see then that the police officers might not have been defeated by the mere ritual invocation of an enemy, but rather for daring to fluctuate in a symbolic universe that they didn't know beyond information, or reason. All faith, although it may be dual and contradictory, must be practiced from the heart, must be sincere.

In the same vein, let's also think of the fearsome Mexican cartel hit men brothers who invoke the Holy Death at the beginning of the third season of *Breaking Bad*. These twins place Heisenberg's portrait on the altar of the so-called "Virgin of the Good Death" and perform a ritual aiming to annihilate Walter White/Heisenberg.

Unfortunately for the twin killers, the aforementioned witchcraft will not succeed.

In the eyes of a rationalist the reasons for this esoteric fiasco are obvious, but if we analyze the fictional phenomenon within the folk cult's logic, one could surmise that the spell did not work because the altar itself had identified the drawing of Heisenberg—placed between black candles—with one of the "partners" of Holy Death or Santa Muerte himself: Jesus Malverde, the magical mustached cowboy, often wearing a hat and always with the looks and style of a fashionable bandit.

The drawing of Heisenberg would have been interpreted by the altar as a mirror or double of Malverde. And such incorporation of the contradictory duality, also shown in the Los Cuates de Sinaloa video clip as a dark mirror interposed between Heisenberg and Jesus Malverde, could also be expressed as a sacred twinning, or as the scientific term "chirality," explained at some point by Walter White himself in his role as the ill-fated chemistry teacher.

That chirality, or contradictory and complementary duality, is manifested throughout the series—even in the picturesque logo of the fast food restaurant "Los Pollos Hermanos"—and is another element tinged with the persistent scent of Coyote mythology, in which the twin of Coyote, the "White Twin", or the "Silver Fox", is often recalled.

### (Simon Magus)

One of the oldest mystical links to contemporary folk saints, that is, to those "miraculous souls" not accepted by the church hierarchy, is the figure of the iconoclastic Simon Magus, the same spirit that one day came to be relied upon by Fauster, the historical Faust, as his guardian angel.

Simon Magus was an early Christian and heretic condemned by the Fathers of the Church because of his vain love for the good life, also deeply hated because he was usually accompanied by Helena, a prostitute, and because of the alleged practice of sexual magic.

One of the most beautiful testimonies on this figure was given by the Serbian writer Danilo Kis in his short story "Simon Magus", a tale that portrays this same Simon's glorious fall from the clouds, the result of a poorly executed trick against the hideous Peter the Apostle: we speak, as expected, of the old though difficult trick of rising in the air.

According to some folklorists, the cult of Simon Magus survives in Central America—where it would have arrived, of course, by means of colonialism—

thanks to its central figure's syncretic transformation to San Simon/Maximón, a folk saint who would blend certain alchemical features of this Simon Magus of early Christianity with the mystique of an ancient Mayan deity: the Ri Laj Mam, the old man, the powerful Promethean grandfather of indigenous Guatemalans.

And certainly it would not hurt to remember that North-American Indians also call "Old Man" the human characterization of Coyote.

### (Francis and the Wolf and Heisenberg)

But let's focus a little on one of the official saints who behaves mostly like a folk saint, St. Francis of Assisi, the saint invoked by Pope Jorge Bergoglio who, according to legend, comes to negotiate with the "evil" represented by a big bad wolf plaguing the community.

When San Francisco asks the angry crowd not to kill the wolf, claiming that he can go into the forest to negotiate with the beast, he is shaping a fable that seems to suggest a relationship with the evil that inhabits our inner forest: instead of a hopeless battle, we should negotiate with it, find a place for it to breathe—art, a television series?—without causing further damage to our comrades, or at least reduce such harm to the minimum acceptable level.

It is interesting, moreover, that in the current Catholic imaginary, two popes co-exist: one that has retired to reflect on the most recent sins of the Church and one that is trying to reform the inveterate institution by way of a pious self-criticism that is capable of bringing a little light into dark areas. Inquisition and Liberation Theology, although remixed and reloaded for the 21st Century. And note that Pope Francis (who would have thought?) also has some similarities with Heisenberg: both suffer from lung problems—Walter White has cancer and Jorge Bergoglio has only one lung—and both have training in chemistry. Sometimes coincidences or synchronicities simply have their own sense of humor.

Heisenberg in park Hasenheide, Berlin Neukölln.

## The face of chaos

The folk saints are often edgewalkers, like coyotes. And it is also true that many of them look a bit like Heisenberg: they are usually depicted with a goatee and/or mustache, sometimes wearing hats and sunglasses, often dressed in black, with the attributes of mystics, bandits or witches, and sometimes possessing androgynous features as well.

In the case of Maximón/San Simon, he might be represented wearing makeup or as a masked man, another feature that relates him with the Coyote of the American Indians, who is often depicted with clown masks.

It is noteworthy that a variety of Maximón figurines have faces that are even reminiscent of the mocking mask of Guy Fawkes, the sixteenth century British rebel, honored in the comic-turned-film *V for Vendetta* by Alan Moore.

From reality to fiction and back to reality. The famous Anonymous mask is based on Guy Fawkes' facial features, and in the contemporary world has become recognized as the true face of chaos. The mask symbolizes everything that there is to fear from a hacker-coyote: you never know what to expect from these individuals. The mask makes its wearers unpredictable, always ready to make a fool of the powerful with their twisted humor and their ability to cross moral boundaries. These are the very same qualities that make folk saints like Maximón generally beloved by the common people and feared by the elite.

Guy Fawkes was an English activist for religious freedom who in 1606 was hanged on the gallows after being convicted of having been part of the incendiary "Gunpowder Plot" seeking to dismantle British power structures of the time using explosives. It is symbolic that annually, on November 5, Guy Fawkes is burned in effigy thousands of times over in England to mark the failure of his incendiary feat, although this festival always leaves an aftertaste of celebration of the dissident's moral victory.

We are talking here about a pyromaniac parade very similar to the traditional burning and/or hangings of Judas in Latin America (incidentally, during Holy Week in Guatemala, Maximón is confused with Judas Iscariot).

This fire party also bears some relationship to the psychedelic annual Burning Man event in the United States. We might even go so far as to say that the burning of Guy Fawkes exhibits certain similarities with the barbaric Mexican torture of the possum, organized year after year in Yucatan—keeping up the futile effort to punish or bring into line our collective trickster, the cheater inside all of us, the Enemy, our heretic, our traitor.

Or we can see that piñata-torture from another vantage point: perhaps, by punishing the possum, the community gets to unleash repressed impulses that at any moment could be directed against their own agents of change. It is perhaps a way of precaution, as they say, preventing themselves from destroying their most precious items in the tortuous path to survival. The same might be said of the annual Guy Fawkes burning.

## Diego Duende

And now a final question: is it a mere coincidence that, during the actual/fake funeral of Walter White in Albuquerque, someone directed a prayer to Federico García Lorca's duende?

The possible transformation of the same gipsy "duende" by the Central American syncretism into "Diego Duende", a frequent altar companion to San

Simon/Maximón, is just another significant synchronicity that gives meaning to these inquiries.

Guy Fawkes/Anonymous in the 8th
District, Vienna.

# Coyote: shape shifter

Coyote is the master of transformations. He is one of the most gifted.

Coyote is considered a sacred animal because American Indians see him as the living intersection between a dog, a fox and a wolf.

Interestingly, not long ago a weird animal was found in the United States that, after genetic analysis, proved to be a hybrid dog, coyote and wolf.

It was not a coyote but it was a Coyote, so to speak, and at this point we all can clearly grasp this strange logic. It is the chaotic logic of nature that suddenly erupts with extreme violence into the orderly appearance of the world.

*Popol Vuh* states that the hero twins Hunahpú and Ixbalanqué triumph thanks to their transformation.

As already mentioned, on their second journey to Xibalba—from which they emerge triumphant—the magic twins are transformed into coyote and opossum. They enter the realm of shadows dressed as beggars, they advance dancing and playing tricks, they are magic tricksters performing magic tricks.

At some point the book even suggests the twins have darkened their skin and their eyes are wider and rounder than usual. Here we might imagine the Mayan twins as characters in the novel *Men of Maize*, from Guatemalan Literature Nobel Prizewinner Miguel Angel Asturias, which are animals and humans and spirits and sometimes even inanimate objects, all at the same time. We can think of them as entities flashing between all these conditions, in an absolute liminal state.

Forthcoming attractions: Kurosawa resurrects and films *Men of Maize*.

In Aztec mythology, meanwhile, it is the famous Quetzalcoatl who displays shape-shifter features. Quetzalcoatl is not only both snake and eagle, as is well known, but also has an evil twin, Tezcatlipoca, who can be depicted as a black jaguar or a coyote. The folk hero Quetzalcoatl also suffers another fractal cut in the form of the axolotl (a-xolotl: water dog, or water coyote, or water monster) that constitutes an immature, failed transformation, or one caught in perpetual larval stage.

In the contemporary global culture of late capitalism, as Fredric Jameson would say, we can find many examples of shape-shifters. Some might say that the transformation of appearance is a quality increasingly in vogue thanks to, or as a result of, digital technologies. Dress up your own selfie.

It is noteworthy that in recent times some of the most iconic shape shifters of our day have bid this world farewell: Michael Jackson, Lou Reed, David Bowie, the artist formerly known as Prince and Juan Gabriel recently ascended to heaven aboard their golden media chariots.

They have now achieved transformation into idols, almost global folk saints, in death. But the most important thing for those of us left living to understand is that all of these artists reacted against, played with, and problematized their own biological gender. It could even be said that, during their lifetimes, they actively hacked key aspects of what the Western popular mass culture considered to be *feminine*.

Let's take a look at David Bowie, who also used to appear associated with his faux twin, the actress Tilda Swinton. He ended his days transforming himself *Bowie* into a black star and from his fluorescent ashes Lady Gaga emerged as a beautiful bird of the new time. This shape-shifter *par excellence* shone as she sang Bowie's songs in the post-mortem tribute at the 2016 Grammy Awards: hack and counter-hack.

We should note also that one of the ancient bearded tricksters, the sprawling Loki, is also known because he can be transformed into a woman. This capability was further illustrated by another shape-shifter media star of our time: the Austrian singer Conchita Wurst, an androgynous Coyota who redeemed the bearded woman known from circus freak-shows.

The use of masks by Anonymous rises to the occasion of the transformative possibilities inherent in our time, in part because the Anonymous mask can conceal a woman, a man who happens to feel like a woman, an Asian or a blond or a black transvestite, or a redheaded male. These masks work at times like the Gorgons instilling fear behind enemy lines of the rigid patriarchy. The mask can be used by a transsexual, or by a girl who begins to feel like a boy.

Collage showing tricksters in
Volkspark Friedrichshain, Berlin.

But the current figure giving most fully-realized form
to this marriage between hacker culture and gender
shape-shifting is heroic whistleblower Chelsea Manning (formerly known as Bradley Manning), an ex-
ceptional person who fulfilled her duty by "betray-
ing" the US Army and the horrors it perpetrated during her military career. In so doing, she faced, on be-
half of all of us, the most powerful war machine in
history. In return, we should be doing everything
possible to get her out of prison.

In the symbolic field some great small victories
arise: Mary Magdalene has recently been raised by
the Church's canon to the category of Christ's disci-
ple. Her spiritual merits had always been indis-
putable; however, macho culture had been very effective in blocking her passage to the high shrines.
That's a big step for the church of Pope Francis, but
not yet one giant leap for mankind.

Perhaps we need more chaos to bring forth further
changes. Because chaos does have its goddesses, and
we ignore them at our peril.

These goddesses of chaos are showing signs of anger.

It's like the Tibetan Dakini dancing on the corpse of a man. Dakini, skydancer, skywalker, advances along her terrifying trajectory through the unconscious regions of the mind, where all the obstacles that will manifest later on our way remain, all those hindrances that come as a result of our still-rejected desires.

If you are strong enough to keep up the pace, the Dakini will free you of all obstacles. She will kill your curses. She knows how to transform the poison into pharmakon but this only happens if one can endure a passage through the unconscious, both personal and collective. Her transit is very painful; almost no one supports it. This goddess of chaos and anger carries the ego's head in one hand. She drinks blood as if it were a Bloody Mary. Like the Hindu goddess Kali, the Dakini dances on the collapsed past.

Perhaps all the goddesses are angry because they've been removed from their positions. The gods of patriarchy have succeeded for a long time in relegating them to the shadows, refusing to recognize their role in the creative cosmic chaos.

This same chaos brings us news of an old shapeshifter from the Maya pantheon: the jaguar goddess Ix Chel who weaves herself and takes the form of a spider.

That really makes you want to borrow for a moment the strings. Hexenspiel: let's weave those string figures of which Donna Haraway has spoken:

What about the role of filmmaker Laura Poitras in this global mobilization of whistleblowers?

Without Wikileaks journalist Sarah Harrison, things would have been very different for Edward Snowden.

Edward Snowden's tweet celebrating that the American $20 bill will from now on bear the face of the heroine, fugitive and black outlaw Harriet Tubman represents just a single tribute to the creative transtemporal energy of women pushing forward the struggles for freedom, for information and knowledge.

The efforts of all these women are guided by Anansi, the African trickstress weaving the spider web of knowledge.

Let us watch her going down to the subconscious underworld, transformed into the Hopi Spider Woman, in order to unearth the fire of human creativity.

Was not Malinche a hacker?

It is not often stated, but the first trickstress to appear in the *Popol Vuh* is Ixkik, princess of the underworld, sentenced to death by her family when they find out she is pregnant by a foreigner.

Ixkik performs a great trick to save her life. She convinces her executors to replace her heart—which the owls have been instructed to bring as a trophy to their Xibalba masters—with a false heart, made from the sap of a tree. The transformation here is a result of art as redemption and it is thanks to this device that Ixkik can then give birth to the androgynous twins that will bring dawn to earth.

Recall the Celtic Brigid, goddess of poetry and the forge. She is the deity of fire but also of words.

There is no doubt that female or matriarchal symbols in our cultural imaginary aren't getting the attention they deserve.

But there are some positive signs. Many Latin American folk saints, despite being the bearers of a tremendous virile energy, usually present one or two androgynous features, and sometimes they even come out as transgender, just like the ancient Aztec god Huehuecoyotl, the "old coyote", or "the very old coyote", a mischievous and dancing spirit able to change his gender at will. The tendency of the folk saints is to be tolerant and even playful in front of all gender and sexual differences and they often are very close on the altars, even contiguous, to powerful female figures such as Santa Muerte, who in particular is seen as their superior, *la mera mera*, the queen.

Maybe these wise spirits are trying to suggest something.

Could it be that the skywalker goddess, who both devastates and heals, has managed to merge with the Mexican folk saint Santa Muerte?

## Guy: Fox

But how could we forget the fox? The beloved Berliner flâneur. The elusive dandy who is its own fox fur bomber jacket.

Anyone who has caught a glimpse of a fox in the middle of the city feels instantly anointed, or chosen.

And maybe they are.

The fox is a scoundrel that slides like a ninja from the forests into our parks, is the ghostly invader of our garages. This little bandit knows how to infiltrate our peaceable, almost abandoned vacation houses: she does her thing with landfills or stored food supplies, runs pranks that we'll try to reconstruct as the puzzle of a crime.

The most beautiful fox would kill our chickens with pleasure if we had chickens. Occasionally some foxy restless lady digs her sharp teeth into the neck of a cat or a small dog, but it just does not matter: our permanent fantasy is that the fox becomes a pet, the children's pet. We ponder the possibility of ordering one of those domesticated fox cubs Russian scientists have created. They're so cute.

A fox may not be as unpopular as a coyote in suburban areas of Los Angeles or New Mexico, let's put it that way, but there are those who want to kill him, or throw him out of the cities, at least. You have to see it to believe it: the little beast has its free predators among us, including those who hunt it for their fur, because they view it as pest control, or (in the cases of poorer predators) because it competes with them for food.

fox
respect

Then there are those who simply respect the fox as it is. They know it's not a toy for family recreation, recognizing it instead as an animal shaman and a cunning and unforgiving predator from which one could learn.

The fox is a messenger of the implicate order of nature. Its animal energy runs parallel to our civilized reality. It carries within itself the task of communicating an intelligence that vibrates in another wave frequency and is expressed through its body.

Fox tattoo in Hufelandstrasse, Berlin
Prenzlauer Berg.

To understand the universe encapsulated inside the body of the fox you can take a look at a meme that has been circulating over social media, in which one of the most anticlimactic moments of Lars von Trier's *Antichrist* is portrayed.

In this scene, actor William Defoe walks desperate through the forest, plagued by the metaphysical fear that saturates the story. Defoe moves in slow motion when suddenly he runs into a dead fox with its guts exposed. The fox revives before his eyes and utters this crucial phrase: "Chaos reigns".

This meme is often shared through social networks to joke about complicated or hopeless situations.

And there the fox's message on the (dis)order of the world is revealed and summarized. Chaos is our nature, the hidden source of our food. This scene from Lars von Trier reinterprets a transcultural mythology.

The sallqa Indians of Peru, for example, speak of a fox in whose womb the seeds of life would be cooked. The fox incubates in its very being the fire of imagination that cooks the food we get from nature.

In the Maya book *The Annals of the Cakchiquel* is said that the first sacred food, the first maize plant, the first corn, emerged from the belly of a coyote.

Let's remember the name of the greatest Aztec poet, "Nezahualcoyotl", means "hungry coyote". The universe is digested in the coyote and fox's womb. This image also brings to mind the poem by Peter Blue Cloud:

*Coyote, Coyote, please tell me – why is Creation?*
Creation is because I
went to sleep last night
with a full stomach,
and when I woke up
this morning,
everything was here.

And there are many more original versions and variations of this von Trier scene.

The secret language of our universe is chaos. This is the essential message the fox/coyote has for us.

Japanese foxes, called kitsune, come to have nine tails when they become evolved Pokémon, the same way that they become "saints"—female, male, or androgynous—who will receive offerings in the real world, and then they adopt the name Inari.

In Bolivia the indigenous pictured the fox as a Promethean being going up to heaven in order to steal fundamental seeds. The seeds of knowledge, it is understood. "Uncle fox" is seen as a hacker of knowledge. He rises to the heavens of the World Wide Web to bring the fruits of creative commons, of open knowledge. Information as a common good.

In the *Popol Vuh* of the Maya-K'iche's there are four animals playing the role of messengers that guide to the riches of nature.

They are the ones who guide humanity towards the encounter with corn: the raven, parrot, coyote and fox.

One of the first attacks Anonymous prepared was on Fox News, the news of the great mass-medial fox. Some of the mythology of Renard the Fox is apparent in *Mr. Fox* by Roald Dahl and Wes Anderson.

And who can forget Diego de la Vega, El Zorro (The Fox), that shrewd swordsman who defends the weakest in multiple movies set in colonial Los Angeles?

Mask and more masks, from El Zorro to Anonymous and on to the implied dynamic Dread Pirate Roberts' character from the novel *The Princess Bride*, whose clothing is nearly identical to El Zorro's and who in turn gave rise to the *nome de guerre* of the creator of Silk Road, one of the most controversial alternative routes to the official Internet, where legal and illegal are in a state of permanent uncertainty. Dread Pirate Roberts is a name used by several unidentified persons. It can be passed from one person to another. No one is Dread Pirate Roberts and Dread Pirate Roberts are all, both in the novel by William Goldman and over the trade routes of the Silk Road. The fox walks over the silk road wearing velvet gloves.

Fox, the animal, has red hair just like Pedro de Alvarado, reputed as the cruelest conqueror. Some say his spirit is embedded in the wood from Maximón itself.

Good and evil are intertwined. And they are also contained in the name of the fox:

The successful German musician Peter Fox (redheaded like a fox) has warmly welcomed a refugee family into his own house.

Vicente Fox is the same Mexican politician who overturned the PRI's quasi-dictatorial power. Then he himself became the president who opened the national resources to US multinationals.

Amarilis Fox, an ex-CIA agent, says in a YouTube video: listen to your enemy. The enemy always sees himself as Luke Skywalker and sees you as Darth Vader.

Foxes always embody crossroads entities. The fox is an edgewalker, it flashes on the threshold of good and evil.

The fox is the false preacher in all those medieval paintings.

We have seen many times that the fox represents the devil or dark forces. The Nazi Desert Fox is one of these satanic invocations.

But life is not a bowl of cherries. We have to understand the dark side of Coyote. He is a Joker. The court jester. The Slipknot Jester. The tycoon-turned-politician Donald Trump, a variation of Stephen King's Pennywise, shows a lack of control and a dark, twisted humor both typical of Coyote.

The Internet is also the great, insatiable fox. You can look at it as a giant beast that wants to consume all of our creativity, and our intelligence as well. But the cycle of predator and prey always reconfigures itself. The fox is a predator today and tomorrow will escape from his superior, the wolf, or will avoid human traps. The next day the rabbit will outsmart the fox and get away: it is a cosmic cycle.

At six years old, Margaret Atwood created super alien flying rabbits that defied the evil foxes. Their planet: Mischiefland.

For the fox's enemy is the rabbit. When in doubt, ask former US President Jimmy Carter, who was attacked by a rabid rabbit during a memorable boat ride. They say it was the most evil trickster incarnation ever. This story, perhaps apocryphal, in which a white killer swimming swamp rabbit tries to reach the former most powerful man on earth, sowing panic among the boat's crew, became a source of rather unexpected political mischief, a wonderful prank of nature.

Rabbits have a reputation for being adorable. That's why it was so incredibly scary.

## Magical Mystery Tour

After a cosplay and furry fandom festival, a boy, still disguised as Frank, the demon rabbit from the film *Donnie Darko*, wandered aimlessly through the beautiful streets of Vienna's seventh district. He was lost among his disjointed thoughts until, at some point, he simply decided to go and get some schnapps.

He walked (or should I say hopped?) half a block and went into a pub called the Voodoo Lounge in the Siebensterngasse.

It was very dark in there, as if it really was a voodoo room.

The bunny boy was shocked by the skulls and other terrifying figures—among them the Baron Samedi—that hung everywhere. However, at the same time he felt that perhaps this atmosphere of false black magic would allow him to go unnoticed.

Mistaken, needless to say. Sooner rather than later a rather tall guy, burly and pale, wearing a hat and black coat, approached him and sat beside him at the bar.

"Are you the walrus?" he asked.

"Hehe. I see what you did there," replied the boy. "I'm the silver rabbit that haunts Donnie Darko. Don't you know the film?"

"It was a rhetorical question, dear. Everyone knows that the walrus was John Lennon. The rabbit was George Harrison, we know this 'cause—"

"I wish I was George Harrison! The mystical Beatle," replied the boy nervously while knocking back a drink. "My name is Diego Reynoso, mucho gusto. I am an anthropology student and a digital rights activist.

And of course, in my spare time I happen to don this furry figure."

"I see," said the man in the black hat, with an ironic gesture. "It's funny because just this morning," he added, "I dreamed that a rabbit escaped the chase. There was a fox that was about to catch it and I fucked everything up. I just wanted to take a picture of the fox, it was a beautiful red one. Then I must have made a wrong move, or took a misstep, the thing is I alerted the bunny unintentionally. The fox looked back at me, we made eye contact, and the rabbit took the opportunity to slip away."

"Very interesting. I'm not sure if you are aware that your dream is clearly the mythical fox-rabbit cycle," said the boy.

"Wow," replied the man in black, scratching his beard. "I never would have imagined. Look, dear, if I were looking for interpretations for my dreams I would pay my psychotherapist a visit, don't you think? I told you the story just because you're hiding inside of that stupid animal costume. Small talk, say. And by the by, you're already too old for these little games, aren't you?"

"I regret to inform you, respectable gentleman, that cosplay is a philosophy of life," replied the boy with dignity. "Doctoral research has been done and Ted Talks have been given on the subject."

"Well, well, big boy, Ted conferences these days are all built up on shit," said the man, taking a sip from his bottle of Coke: "Fuck me."

"Please understand, my dear sir, I practice cosplay because it is an effective way to achieve samadhi. Don't you know what that is? I do this because I received a spiritual orientation. I have been instructed to represent this rabbit until I find my essence. Aleister Crowley made the samadhi contemplating the god Pan. My soul is that of a trans-species being. Don't you know what that is? The trans-species philosophy teaches us that our human body is nothing but a cover for an animal spirit. I'm actually a rabbit trapped in the body of a man."

And so on and so on and so on. And so on and so on and so on. And so and so on and so on. And so on and so on and so on.

So the boy continued talking and talking for half an hour. No one had ever given him the opportunity to express himself so deeply. Let's say the man in the hat had pushed a button.

And so on and so on and so on. And so on and so on and so he continued his monologue for another twenty minutes. The bunny boy was in ecstasy. He felt like a Ted Talk Guru. He wanted to record himself—sadly, he had forgotten his smartphone at home. This bunny boy is always so distracted.

Healing ceremony: rabbit staring at
the falling snake.

While talking about this aloud, he fully recognized that his identity was precisely that of a rabbit wearing a stupid human suit. "Now the best I can do is one last drink and then leave," he said.

Then he asked for the bill. By that time he had already forgotten his interlocutor in the black coat. Not finding him in the seat next to him, he thought he might have gone to the bathroom.

The bartender told him his total. The boy paid it and left the Voodoo Lounge striding as if someone were after him.

That same bartender, a man in his fifties, a plump blonde with some half-Gypsy features, ended his shift twenty minutes after the rabbit boy had settled up.

It was one of those evenings when he just wanted to leave work, get home, take off his shoes, open an aromatic bottle of red wine, eat a plate of pasta and relax listening to the Beatles. It was a more than a perfect plan, especially because it was easy to fulfill.

Later, during the tasty ravioli dinner he himself prepared, the bartender would remark with his wife —without giving it much importance—the curious story of that crazy customer in a rabbit costume, arguing vehemently with a stupid black hat placed on a chair.

# Operation: Rabbit

In an episode titled "Operation: Rabbit," one of the most acclaimed tricksters of all time, the hilarious Bugs Bunny, shows us the key to avoiding the hungry Wile E. Coyote: we must humor him, pay lip service to him, let him have his way, let him believe that he has everything under control.

Wile E. Coyote has business cards that describe him as a genius.

*Wile E. Coyote: Genius.*

Bugs Bunny knows of the great scientific intelligence that Coyote boasts—so similar in this to Walter White—so he plays into this side of him. He recognizes his genius. Bugs tricks Wile E. by validating the greatness of his ideas and using this seesaw he gets out of his hands again and again.

He knows that beyond his intelligence Coyote is governed by appetite. At some point Wile E. Coyote tries to catch the lucky rabbit using a sexy female bunny robot. For the unlucky *Canis latrans*, it turns out Bugs has also invented a cyber-coyota, which becomes a tool to unleash Wile E. Coyote's unbridled sexual fury.

Fight fire with fire, Bugs Bunny says. He can be a mad scientist as well.

Bugs Bunny has given up being the scapegoat. He just wants to get away with it. He does not want to become the hero of the story, much less the victim, except in the rare occasions that he becomes a victim of himself. At the end of the day Bugs is also a coyote. The episode "Operation: Rabbit" brings to mind the taste of the popular tales of Uncle Rabbit and Uncle Coyote, distributed all over the Americas.

Memorable is the compilation of these short stories prepared by the Nicaraguan poet Pablo Antonio Cuadra, the same one who wrote, by the way, some clever notes on the Nicaraguan trickster: "El Güegüense", whose name means, oh surprise, "The Old Man", and is also called "Macho Ratón", that is, "Macho Mouse".

The rabbit and coyote cycle, or the fox and rabbit cycle, always puts us at the edges of wild intelligence, wit, and the moods we all need to survive. Coyote and rabbit, fox and rabbit form a dialectical unity, a sort of animal yin and yang.

Maybe this is why in the German Rumpelstilzchen legend, it is said that the protagonist's salvation can be found in the same spot in the forest where the fox and rabbit meet. And please don't forget this girl protagonist progresses towards the desired social mobility.

Perhaps the same is suggested by the recent animated film, *Zootopia*, in which the fox, a natural-born bandit, and the noble, persistent and adaptable police bunny girl learn to be friends and to work together. Such reconciliation may represent the ideal merging of the contradictory trickster powers in our psyche.

Rabbit in park Hasenheide, Berlin
Neukölln.

# Little Jack wanders through Neverland

It is often said that hackers, just like Wile E. Coyote, are touched by genius.

It's funny because this has positioned hackers in a liminal zone of our cultural imagination. They now occupy a space normally reserved for great artists or scientists, although the latter are considered "mad scientists" if they are too eccentric.

The issue here is that referring to hackers as geniuses has strained them. But we will return to this a little later.

First let's talk about an artistic genius.

Salvador Dalí, the great Spanish surrealist, never hesitated to call himself a genius. He did it with such grace that the display of vanity was not only acceptable but enjoyable, even necessary; that was what everyone expected from Dalí at the end of the day.

Here the little hypothesis is that Salvador Dalí could afford such outbursts because he modeled himself after the legendary Hermes, the trickster messenger of the gods. Dalí himself acknowledges this plot in a couple of videos that can be found on YouTube.

Salvador Dalí even says that he is the embodiment of Hermes. Once, when a reporter reminds him that he's often accused of being a clown, Dalí says that he does not care, he's indeed a clown, or Harlequin, synonymous with Hermes: "the incarnation of Hermes by Mercury, the huckster, makes me a clown, that is, a harlequin."

Angelologist Michel Serres identifies Hermes and Harlequin as miscegenation symbols, for he thinks of philosophy and art as patchwork just like the harlequin costume.

Salvador Dalí is a clown in the same way the American Indian Coyote becomes a clown wearing a clown mask. Coyote is also a harlequin clown incarnating the cosmic huckster that sees us from the Clown Nebula.

Not long ago, the Mexican newspaper *La Jornada* published an interview with "the last living surrealist," Pedro Friedenberg (also Mexican), who denies slyly that he is a clown, while claiming to be a contemporary of Copernicus and posing for the photograph wearing a Guy Fawkes mask.

Let us not forget the world map in the fool's head, the jester, attributed to Renaissance mathematician and gnomonic Orontius Finaeus Delphinatus.

The tarot starts with the No. 0, the fool's card.

It is the Joker's insane genius that wants to discipline the closet homosexual, millionaire and uppity vigilante who goes by the name "Batman".

Joker will not stop fucking with him until he accepts his shadow and gets out of the Batcave, or at least until he stops chasing his own inner Joker.

Joker energy is voracious and dangerous; just remember this was the second to last role played by Heath Ledger, who later committed suicide.

The Joker, according to what Ledger declared to the press, is what sunk him in depression.

Interestingly, during his last and unfinished role, Heath Ledger was characterized as "Tony the liar," a trickster and clownish amnesiac, who comes in as a hangman who brings to mind the hanging Judas Iscariot: the scapegoat.

The evil clown, Pennywise, looks to bust you right where your more repressed fears lie, your traumas. He slips into your dreams to turn them into nightmares just like Freddy Krueger, or a foolish Sandman.

Another meme circulating on social media shows Donald Trump all dressed and made up as the Joker; the Joker, that character that feeds on our most basic fears, the most hidden but persistent of human desires. The Joker wants to dominate the world while crazily dancing with the collective shadow.

By the way, don't you have the impression sometimes that memes are the voice of the chaotic and collective wisdom of Coyote?

Memes are the tiniest possible display of the great cosmic joke.

One literary visionary—blind and Argentinian—once said that the universe may well be a cosmic joke.

And then another one—American and a tennis player—took this joke seriously, got some inspiration from Shakespeare, and wrote a novel of over a thousand pages: thus he became the imp who wrote an infinite jest.

Silly jokes taken seriously can also be a work of genius: Till Eulenspiegel, just like the Chapulín Colorado, twists foolishly the proverbs to extract their true occult wisdom.

It is often said that hackers are fools. Hackers are nerds and nerds are fools.

The nerdy schoolgirl who lives in an absurd state of being the smartest and the dumbest at the very same time.

She is the Beatles' fool on the hill.

The woman of a thousand voices talking perfectly clear but nobody listens. The song says something like that.

It's the same guy who played the clown in class to keep from being bullied. Or to forget that his father wasn't paying even the slightest attention to him.

Becoming Coyote is a survival strategy incorporated in all of us.

Even among philosophers: consider Slavoj Žižek as the histrionic thinker who came from the underworld.

Žižek's joke: who would have thought that Western philosophy was to find one of its best critics and its best spokesman in a Slovenian thinker?

Slavoj Žižek, genius and harlequin, the Elvis of philosophy, gives the impression that he is fighting an inner imp as intelligent as he is. This imp jumps and kicks, but remains inside his body.

This is the same fight referred by the Spanish poet Federico García Lorca in his famous theory of duende.

Lorca explains the telluric energy that makes an artist an artist. On the other hand a very talented person is not always an artist. The great mystery that makes something work and at the same time makes something almost the same won't work: the duende, the imp.

Lorca explains that the fight with this ancient energy buried within us is what allows the emergence of a true work of genius.

When something is really good you say "it has duende".

One here thinks about the great Brazilian singer Tim Maia, who one day, apparently heard the voice of duende, dressed as Hermes Trismegistus, and decided to go out and search for him.

Tim Maia took "o caminho do bem", the right path, left the vicious life and became a devout follower of the great Hermes Trismegistus.

During this period he recorded what perhaps will be remembered as his best album, or at least his album with duende: *Rational Culture*.

After this recording, however, Tim Maia would not be the same. He did not record anything of great value afterwards. Everything indicates that the duende had won.

Something similar may have happened with another Brazilian virtuoso, Arnaldo Baptista, who left his successful band Os Mutantes due to drug abuse and fights with his fellow musicians.

Baptista reached a solo recording, the wonderful 1974 album *Loki?*, with a theme that speaks for itself: "Voce tá pensando que eu sou Loki, bicho". *You're thinking that I'm Loki, kiddo.* Some years later Baptista was interned in a psychiatric hospital. Made it out after a while, attempted suicide included.

And what about Syd Barret and his sudden abandonment of Pink Floyd? Has the piper Pan, the faun, blurred his mind just at the gates of dawn?

Mushrooms and LSD are the trolls and pranksters of the brain.

Little man conducts the orchestra. It's the hobgoblin that releases chaos in *A Midsummer Night's Dream*.

Psychedelics gurus often come into contact with goblins, leprechauns, kobolds, and many more variants.

Some say that genius often comes when one follows the trasgo, the imp or goblin that transgresses the limits.

Sometimes a mutually beneficial agreement with this imp is achieved, as in the case of the Haitian writer Dany Laferrière who recognizes in Legba, the trickster of the Yoruba, the one who is responsible for his good fate as a writer.

Or in the case of Robert Johnson who went beyond the Faustian myth, becoming the blues genius thanks to his encounter with the devil.

On the other hand, for the ancient Romans, genius was a childbirth allowance. Everyone is born with genius, quite like the idea of nahual of the Maya. Genius is an internal little duende. It's every individual's responsibility to wake it up.

But as already said, this is dangerous. The imp can take full control. Then he requires you to become Peter Pan wearing its winged shoes like the shoes of Hermes.

Michael Jackson never got out of Neverland.

Jackson is the son of Jack.

Listen to that voice-over telling us Tyler Durden is Jack's broken heart.

For some it seems pretty obvious that the character of English folklore called "Jack in the Green," with its strange feast of drunken bushes and practical jokes, is a disguised version of Puck, or Robin Hood himself.

Jacob is the biblical trickster. Jacob is always playing tricks on his brother Esau in order to position himself higher up on the hereditary chain.

Our dark side is Uncle Jack: the neo-Nazi from *Breaking Bad's* last season.

Heisenberg defeats Uncle Jack, his last and best armed enemy, thanks to a guerrilla trick based on the previous acceptance of his own shadow: yes, all of Walter White's crimes were committed for the sake of pleasure.

Hit the road, Jack Sparrow.

Go follow the path of Santiago and never come back.

Because Jacob also means Santiago. And Jacob also means Diego.

Juan Diego is the Mexican Indian to whom the Virgin of Guadalupe reveals herself.

Diego Maradona scores in one game the most beautiful goal and the trickiest goal of history.

Was it the hand of God or the hand of duende?

Evil and good are always twisted, intertwined.

And what is what unites, apart from their names, San Simon and Simone Biles, the last Olympic gymnastics genius?

What lurks in the mysterious link between the names Maximón, the Guatemalan pagan holy friend of prostitutes and homosexuals, and Maximin, the German teen poet for whom Stefan George lit candles after his death?

The genius of the thousand names produces unexpected connections in the hermeneutical (from Hermes) horizon, and the beautiful dakini interweaves chaotically the fruits of intelligence.

Works of genius are creativity in a state of total freedom. Imagination released, unleashed. Strawberry fields forever.

This intelligence is as fertile as it is dangerous, as we have seen: intelligence released is the rattlesnake.

This is also understood by neoliberalism, which is why corporations have advanced control of and profit from the matter, lest people start thinking for themselves.

Your ideas can topple governments, break down borders, sink presidential campaigns.

That is also why your data is so important.

The Internet is a source of chaos that everyone wants to control.

Master of disaster: Coyote is a teacher who wears the robes of entropy, like that pixie called Poltergeist, a minister officiating chaos in our homes and on our computers.

Let's dance with chaos: try and look for a PDF of *Popol Vuh* online. You will see that at its beginning is a pair of twins who are artists, who are recognized as great silversmiths and craftsmen. They are the half brothers who are always bullying the younger twins, who arrive later, the children of Ixkik: Hunahpú and Ixbalanqué.

They are victims of the arrogance of their elder siblings; however, Hunahpú and Ixbalanqué plot their revenge slowly. They work hard, day and night, until one day they catch their brothers off guard. They play a couple of magic tricks on them and transform them into monkeys. The older siblings, now monkeys, begin to look ridiculous in the eyes of the grandmother: History.

And here we return to the delicate situation alluded to at the beginning of the chapter, in which hackers are being considered geniuses—and also demons, for genius and demons go hand by hand, according to Harold Bloom—affording them a status almost as popular as artists. This should make us see hackers as a new artistic avant-garde, or a certain type of artist who redefines the avant-garde: the supernerds, as explained by the German playwright Angela Richter. Richter has written and directed several plays on hackers and hacker culture, and her thesis is that these supernerds, a bunch of hackers, activists, hacktivists, cypherpunks, whistleblowers and others, can drive social change by taking advantage of the porous boundary between the codifying hacker activity and the artistic avant-garde. At the same time the concept of SuperNerd is an invitation for artists to embrace the hacker culture and take part in the process of social change.

It is not by chance that the Mayan Tzolkin calendar begins in the sign Batz (the monkey) and ends at the nahual Tzi (the coyote). Hunahpú and Ixbalanqué could then be the hero archetypes that evolve through the calendar wheel, the wheel of days, until they reach the field of supernerds, those liminal beings: part avant-garde artists, part geeks misfits and revolutionaries.

But this we do not know it for sure, it is just a guess.

One of the peculiarities of Coyote is that he does not understand whether he is an animal, a god, a superhero or the little Nemo lost in Slumberland. And it is precisely this state of total confusion that gives us the best lessons.

Because genius is also silly, is a fool. It lets itself be swallowed by the whale to emerge, transformed, as *future* Jonah.

Indians say that one day Coyote let himself be swallowed by the giant military-industrial-cybernetic complex that governs and commodifies us.

Or perhaps it was just the giant Moloch of the mind recalled by Ginsberg?

In there, Coyote evolves, matures, grows up. He decides to start stabbing the giant from the inside, while feeding other people also swallowed, and then he's hacking directly into the giant's heart until the giant, in great pain, open his mouth for a short moment.

And then Coyote finally escapes, through the NSA's headquarters.

Tricksters collage in Berlin Friedrichshain.

# Decoding Coyote: further reading

This open-source codex seeks to unite the contemporary traffickers of information with the smoke signals of their totemic animal.

The mission is to decode the big data encrypted in the ancestral body of Coyote and deliver a sparkling report, or perhaps just a colorful set of leaks, that may be of some use, not only to those who are dedicated to the noble profession of hackers and whistleblowers, but also to those who want to learn some of the tricks and masquerades that the meandering Coyote uses to triumph over the trials of the digital, real and imagined underworlds.

This is not a scholarly work; however, what follows is a brief annotated bibliography of some of the sources consulted in order to weave the Harlequin costume:

This book owes its germination impulse, in part, to the "Digital Colonialism" project founded in Berlin by the Guatemalan digital rights activist and lawyer Renata Ávila.

Regarding the current situation of cyberspace, the perspective adopted in this book comes from a variety of texts and interviews from New Media scholars, Internet critics, hacktivists, hackers and whistleblowers such as Tim Wu, Geert Lovink, Alberto Cerda Silva, Evgeny Morozov, Sascha Lobo, Kristian Lukic, Gisela Pérez de Acha, Nanjira Sambuli, Joana Varon, Solana Larsen, Sebastian Christ, Edward Snowden, Jacob Appelbaum and Julian Assange, among others.

When it comes to the First World/Global South tensions in general, the basic framework was provided by the postcolonial and decolonial theories. The emerging field of "digital-postcolonialism" or "postcolonial digital humanities" was also taken under consideration.

With regard to Coyote, this book wants to depict a more or less free interpretation, presenting it as the "fashion-trickster" par excellence, and also as the best metaphor for the mutant ability of the transcultural trickster itself, the very same ability that allows its imagined transformation into multiple contemporary figures.

Nevertheless, if what you want is to deepen your understanding of the traditional American Indian Coyote figure, read *American Indian Trickster Tales (Myths and Legends)* by Richard Erdoes and Alfonso Ortiz, along with Gail Robinson's *Coyote the Trickster* and *The Trickster in Ginsberg: A Critical Reading* by Katherine Campbell Mead-Brewer.

The idea of comparing the hackers with coyotes came by dint of observation, but this work only managed to settle on this intuition thanks to the reading of Gabriella Coleman's essays linking tricksters, trolls and Anonymous.

Moreover, the figure of the coyote as a contemporary theoretical concept appears in some of Donna Haraway's texts, which also contemplates the coyote as a connector between nature and culture, or as a trickster encoder. Similarly, Haraway's definition of the Cyborg as a mutant being between animal, human and the machine has always been an inspiration for this essay.

In a parallel vein, it was in reading the American sociologist Diane Nelson, where the concept of

"Maya-hacker" appears, which led to consider the trickster-hacker relationship from the perspective of the Mayan culture heroes.

With regard to the trickster figure per se, the best course of action would be reading the extraordinary *Trickster Makes This World: Mischief, Myth and Art* by Lewis Hyde, while checking, of course, the seminal works on the subject by Claude Lévi-Strauss.

Besides anthropology, it is important to review the iconic writings of Carl Jung, those of Joseph Campbell, and Vladimir Propp's studies of traditional folktales.

At the most general level, this book pursues a kind of imaginative argument. One of the concepts treasured during the writing was the "chi-xi", created by the Bolivian Aymaran postcolonial thinker Silvia Rivera Cusicanqui, which states the mixing or the miscegenation of images doesn't necessarily imply fusion but rather conflict and complement.

In such wording one should mention once again the French philosopher Michel Serres and his Hermes and Harlequin invocation as vectors of patchwork.

Another tutelary figure of sorts was the Mexican thinker Carlos Monsiváis, who certainly blew from heaven all of his boundless passion for Latin American popular culture and its intersection with global pop.

As for the folk saints, one of the most important influences was the Ecuadorian philosopher Bolívar Echeverria's "theory of Baroque", with its fascinating idea of a new mestizo civilization forged by a native dramatization of the European/conqueror/colonizer order. Echeverría's Baroque even suggests the introduction of the native code in the key code, which alters it and which appropriates it, an idea of ancient hacking that largely guided this text.

In the same note, it is important to take into account the "hybrid cultures" conceived by the Argentinian Nestor García Canclini and the concept of Maximón as "articulator of differences" posed by the Guatemalan sociologist and writer Mario Roberto Morales. No less important was the reading of *The Devil and Commodity Fetishism in South America*, by Michael T. Taussig, and the same goes for the collection of essays entitled *Breaking Bad: 530 gramos de papel para serieadictos no rehabilitados* ("*Breaking Bad: 530 grams of paper for non-rehabilitated series-addicts*"), coordinated by Sergio Cobo and Víctor Hernández-Santaolalla, and also some chapters from the book *Alchemical Mercury: A theory of Ambivalence*, by Karen Pinkus.

From the above we can move on to reading Eric Hobsbawm, mainly his book *Bandits*, which allows us to understand Robin Hood as a substantial "forest-elf" and thus imagine it in connection with social or cultural movements, from the ancient rebel Guy Fawkes to the contemporary use of the mask by Anonymous.

The discussion of the latter topic was also inspired, in part, by some musical or dramatic works such as the *Opera do Malandro* by the Brazilian tropicalist Chico Buarque, a piece which, in turn, comes from the German Bertolt Brecht and Kurt Weill's *The Threepenny Opera*, which in turn was inspired by *The Beggar's Opera* created by the Londoner John Gay: exercises, all of them, in the aesthetic sublimation of thugs and bandits, or their artistic consecration.

On the other hand, for considering the symbolism of masks, the thinking of the Austrian philosopher Thomas Macho provided a significant platform. Specifically, his essay "Second-Order Animals: Cultural Techniques of Identity and Identification" has been taken as a reference.

With regard to the *Popol Vuh*, the basis for this book was the poetic Spanish version translated by the Mayan-K'iche' scholar Luis Enrique Sam Colop. The complex translation by Adrián Inés Chávez, which portrays a rather challenging mystical exploration, was considered as well. The *Popol Vuh*'s English translation by Tedlock was equally consulted.

Beyond Lorca's "teoría del duende" ("theory of duende"), the idea of briefly discussing the notion of genius emerged from the book *Spheres* by the German philosopher Peter Sloterdijk, and perhaps a little bit as well from the recently published Salman Rushdie novel, *Two Years, Eight Months and Twenty-Eight Nights*, where another variant of genius or genies is mentioned: the "jinn".

The concept of "supernerds", meanwhile, is a creation of the German dramatist Angela Richter.

The link between the potential supernerds and the myth of the trickster-twins of the *Popol Vuh* was established as a consequence of reading the Guatemalan Mayan sociologist Saríah Acevedo's essay "La dinámica del cambio social en la concepción maya" ("The dynamics of social change: a Mayan perspective"), where she explains the defeat of the craftsmen-twin-bully-monkeys at hands of the trickster-twin-coyotes.

Fox at Potsdamer Platz, Berlin.

## About the author

Alan Mills was born in Guatemala in 1979. In the past ten years, he has lived in Buenos Aires, São Paulo, Paris, Madrid and Leipzig, and has read at poetry festivals throughout Europe and Latin America. He has lived in Berlin since 2012, where he is writing a dissertation on contemporary Latin American literature, in particular indigenist science fiction. Published works include the books *Marca de agua*, *Síncopes* (also translated into French) and *Pasan poesía en la televisión apagada* and the e-books *Eine Subkultur der Träume. Auf Twitter* and *Hacking Coyote: Tricks on Digital Resistance*. He is on Twitter as @alan1000s. https://twitter.com/alan1000s

## About mikrotext

mikrotext is a digital publisher for short digital and paper reading, founded in 2013 in Berlin. We focus on new literary texts that comment on contemporary questions and allow insights into tomorrow. The texts are inspired by discussions on social media platforms and reflect today's global debates. All texts are published in German, but selected titles will be made available in English. Some ebooks are also available in printed format.

# Catalogue

Abbas, Rasha: *Die Erfindung der deutschen Grammatik. Geschichten*. Aus dem Arabischen von Sandra Hetzl. Februar 2016. Auch erhältlich als gedruckte Ausgabe.

Adrian, Stefan: *Bluffen. Ein Roman*. September 2014.

Adrian, Stefan: *Der Gin des Lebens. Drinklyrik*. Juni 2014.

Alassaf, Assaf: *Abu Jürgen. Mein Leben mit dem deutschen Botschafter*. Aus dem Arabischen von Sandra Hetzl. Oktober 2015.

Bwansi, Patras; Ziemke, Lydia: *Mein Name ist Bino Byansi Byakuleka. Doppel-Essay*. Januar 2015. Auch erhältlich auf Englisch.

Christ, Sebastian: *Berliner Asphalt. Geschichten von Menschen in Kiezen*. Juni 2014.

Christ, Sebastian: *Mein Brief an die NSA. Auf der Suche nach meinen Daten*. Dezember 2013.

Christ, Sebastian: *Ich bin privat hier. Eine Ukraine-Reportage*. Januar 2015.

Cravan, Arthur: *König der verkrachten Existenzen. Best of*. Aus dem Französischen von Hanna Mittelstädt und Pierre Gallissaires. Februar 2016.

Faiz, Julia Tieke: *Mein Akku ist gleich leer. Ein Chat von der Flucht*. April 2015. Auch erhältlich als gedruckte und erweiterte Ausgabe.

Fargo Cole, Isabel: *Ungesichertes Gelände. Liebesnovelle*. Dezember 2013.

Fischer, Jan: *Ihr Pixelherz. Eine Love Story*. Juni 2015.

Fischer, Jan (Hg.): *Irgendwas mit Schreiben. Diplomautoren im Beruf*. März 2014.

Franzobel: *Steak für alle. Der neue Fleischtourismus*. Juni 2013.

Geißler, Heike: *Saisonarbeit. Volte #2*. Dezember 2014.

Gerhardt, Katharina; Kirsten, Caterina; Novel, Ariane; Richter, Nikola; Rudkoffsky, Frank O.; Siegmund, Eva (Hg.): *Willkommen! Blogger schreiben für Flüchtlinge*. Dezember 2015.

Herzberg, Ruth: *Wie man mit einem Mann glücklich wird. Beobachtungen*. August 2015.

Khan, Sarah: *Der Horrorpilz. Eine unbefriedigte Geschichte*. Oktober 2013.

Kluge, Alexander: *Die Entsprechung einer Oase. Essay für die digitale Generation*. März 2013.

Kuhlbrodt, Jan: *Das Elster-Experiment. Sieben Tage Genesis*. Juni 2013.

Mesch, Stefan; Richter, Nikola (Hg.): *Straight to your heart. Verbotene Liebe 1995-2015*. Juni 2015.

Mills, Alan: *Eine Subkultur der Träume. Auf Twitter*. Aus dem Spanischen von Johanna Richter. Dezember 2015.

Palzer, Thomas: *Spam Poetry. Sex der Industrie für jeden*. Juli 2013.

Rinke, Moritz; Roth, Claudia u.a.: *Gezi bleibt. Stimmen zum Aufbruch in der Türkei*. Juli 2013.

Saeed, Aboud: *Der klügste Mensch im Facebook. Statusmeldungen aus Syrien*. Aus dem Arabischen von Sandra Hetzl. März 2013. Auch erhältlich als gedruckte Ausgabe und auf Englisch.

Saeed, Aboud: *Lebensgroßer Newsticker. Szenen aus der Erinnerung*. Aus dem Arabischen von Sandra Hetzl. März 2015. Auch erhältlich als gedruckte Ausgabe.

Sargnagel, Stefanie: *In der Zukunft sind wir alle tot. Neue Callcenter-Monologe*. März 2014. Auch erhältlich als gedruckte und erweiterte Ausgabe.

Zeegen, Chloe: *I love myself ok? A Berlin Trilogy*. Oktober 2013.

**Alan Mills**
**Hacking Coyote**
**Tricks for Digital Resistance**

**a mikrotext**

Editing: Cory Tamler
Pictures: Alan Mills
Cover Design: Andrea Nienhaus
Cover Picture: pixabay.com (Lizenz CC0 1.0)
Fonts: PTL Attention, Gentium Plus
Production: Booktype
Printed in Germany

www.mikrotext.de – info@mikrotext.de

ISBN 978-3-944543-43-7